During elementary school, Lorraine received two Island-wide awards for essay writing and later in high school three awards for English Literature. While intermittently returning to writing, she pursued other creative endeavours and a career in Management, Accounting and Finance.

Lorraine returned to writing through her love for reading and the studies of philosophy and psychology. Her life experiences and observations through professional coaching are documented in two books of poetry. A true-life journey of expressive healing and personal growth designed to inspire the reader.

Lorraine is a Chartered Professional Accountant (CPA) and an Adler Certified Professional Coach (ACPC). She resides in Toronto, Ontario, Canada.

Dedication

This book of poetry, *You in Me,* is dedicated to my mother, Lucy John Grell; and my father, Alexander (Alick) Dorival, both now deceased. Their talents of singing and trumpeting respectively barely touched the surface as they seemed to have been extraordinarily gifted beyond standards of their time. They performed only on the small Caribbean Island, which in their time lacked a wider exposure and global audience. My mother's singing voice still remains one of the most beautiful and versatile I have ever heard, and my father's music was said to have been one of the best on the planet in his days. This is dedicated to such as yet undiscovered extraordinary talents.

Lorraine J. Dorival

You in Me

Poetry of Healing and Growth

Austin Macauley Publishers™
London • Cambridge • New York • Sharjah

Ordering Information
Quantity sales: Special discounts are available on quantity purchases by corporations, associations, and others. For details, contact the publisher at the address below.

Publisher's Cataloging-in-Publication data
Dorival, Lorraine J.
You in Me

ISBN 9798886937190 (Paperback)
ISBN 9798886937206 (ePub e-book)

Library of Congress Control Number: 2023912968

www.austinmacauley.com/us

First Published 2023
Austin Macauley Publishers LLC
40 Wall Street, 33rd Floor, Suite 3302
New York, NY 10005
USA

mail-usa@austinmacauley.com
+1 (646) 5125767

Acknowledgements

My deepest gratitude is to Robert Owen, my cousin-in-law, for his keen listening ear against which I could bounce my ideas. His listening skills captured my song and lyrics and transferred them into a beautiful musical score.

I thank my siblings, Jennifer White, Germaine Rabess, Connie Alleyne, Antoinette Charles-Owen and Gifford Rabess, who are continuously providing me with the learning platform I need to become a better person.

I thank my friend Lorraine Delsol for her kindness and ready generosity in procuring what I need to produce my work.

Table of Contents

Spirituality **13**

Greatness of Life 17

Spiritual Yearning 19

Clearing 21

Selfhood 23

What Is Love 26

Ask and Receive 29

Grace 31

Creativity 33

Consciousness 35

Joy, Joy, Joy 37

The Holy Spirit 39

Spiritual Awakening 41

Spiritual Union 43

Purification 45

Playground of Dreams 47

Life Purpose 49

The Teacher Learner 52

Heart's Desire 54

Public Life 57

Eternal Love 62

Happiness 63

Searching for God 67

Spontaneity 69

Me, Myself and I 71

Mission of Faith 75

Talent 78

Prayer of Faith 79

Fantasy 81

T'ai Chi 85

Homecoming 87

Relationships 91

Life 93

Inclusivity 96

Emotional Intelligence 98

Liking 101

Tes Kawants 103

Imperfection 108

The Elites 110

Siblings 115

Aging 122

Romance 126

Life Lessons 129

Humorous Moments 134

Miramur – The Forest Nymph 137

Glossary **139**

Spirituality

You In Me

Lorraine Dorival

36
S
ther When you speak to me, I hear you and me. Are you my mo - ther?
40
S
Am I, your bro-ther or are you an - o - ther too close to the o - ther?
44
S
When I'm close to you, I can sense your need. My need calls to yours, it's the
48
S
same old deed we share to - ge - ther hold - ing hands with each o -
52
S
ther. As we fill our needs, I sense you and me.

Greatness of Life

What greater bliss
Than unity with the divine!
What greater love
Than the sharing of pain!
What greater good
Than common sense of purpose!
What greater joy
Than knowledge of the source.

How potent the grace
Of wisdom ever knowing.

How clear the vision,
Perceiving the shift
From intensive pain
To all-encompassing love,
To joy, to nothing.

A well-spring of grace,
Transforming struggles to love
Then joy, then nothing.
No thing! No thing!

And a return to something.
The ego.
Yours, mine, ours.

Never-ending, never-ending.

A realm of inexhaustibility.

Spiritual Yearning

How my spirit longs for freedom.
To bathe in morning sunlight
And touch the dewy grass.
To linger midst the flowers
And chirps of merry birds
As they hop from branch to branch.

How my spirit longs for silence,
Broken only by pouring rain
And the gush of lively streams,
As they wind their joyous ways.

How my spirit longs for peace
Like a babe asleep in fleece.
As I watch the expanse of ocean
And miles of sandy beach.

How my spirit longs to love
From a pulsing heart of joy,
With bliss overwhelming,
Vibrating the entire being.

My craving soul,
In loving and giving
Must thee express
Its needs for freeing.

Clearing

A long, simple lilac satin shift,
A gayly coloured turban lift
Adorned her slim figure as she
Approached my bedroom door.

In vain were my attempts to protest.
Appeals soundless and motionless
Were pushed back and suppressed.
Like a dummy, I cowed in the bed.

Go away was my silent command.
Taking no heed, she sternly demand,
Then emerged with a giant cart
Piled with bags, baskets and crates.

All closets and drawers were cleansed.
From where did she find so much dense?
When surplus had already been disposed
From seemingly already empty tents?

Protesting silently and motionlessly,
Laying stuck in bed dispassionately,

She took away my good store-a-ways
Which were not in line for giveaways.

She pushed the cart out of the door,
Taking away all my personal fare.
Leaving the rooms empty and bare.
Clearing and cleaning my living lair.

Her actions were a total surprise.
Clearing space could lessen my demise.
She knew I was carrying some baggage.
And needed help to ease the luggage.

Baggage keeps me utterly lifeless,
Unmotivated and unresponsively listless,
Difficult to shake off and self-drive.
Unable to purposefully arrive.

Cleansing and clearing my living space,
Diminished my heavy stifling disgrace.
I gradually felt bathed, light and free
Like a gigantic weight lifted off my feet.

With head space unencumbered,
Light heartedness so long desired,
Vision clear and movement free,
My mind in a whirl of acceptance.

Selfhood

Your thoughts about me,
Reflect thinking of yourself,
Projected unawares unto me,
Are similar thoughts of you.

Each being is complete
With small differences.
Each being is unique
With some peculiarities.

With slightness in stature,
Gentleness in demeanour,
And honesty in nature,
My sleeve wears my heart
Like a badge of honour.

My life carves its seasons.
Detracts the winter blues,
Sucks the summer sunshine,
Wearing autumn colours,
Bloomed by spring showers.

I am vulnerable and real,
Make no pretence of being,
Deflecting slight untruths,
And rolling with the punches.

Truth rings out in my pain
And the silence of my moods.
Joy sings out in my songs
And the pureness of my voice.

I am visible and present.
Do not ignore my cries.
Reserve your judgement,
Until the truth decries.

When joyously released,
Laugh out loud with me.
Sing, dance and give praise,
Such are fleeting moments.

A mind prone to learning,
Searching the unattainable.
Knowing more becomes less
Of life stream sustainable.

My spirit dwells in reality.
Transgressions are forgiven,
Oozing strength and courage
And resilience to the future.

Angels uphold me always
Saying, “There’s nothing to fear.
You will not crumple and fall.
We hold your life dear.”

My inner child released
Victimization and strain.
Longing and willing to love
And freely roam again.

I am a creation of mankind.
See me as you see yourself.
Know me as a way of learning
Much more about yourself.

One spirit, One love, All one.

What Is Love

Love is a feeling of completeness,
Fulfilment and appreciation which
Leaves a warm fuzz of afterglow.

A mother gives birth to her young.
A father holds his babe the first time
And both give nurturing to the baby.

Slipping a hand with tenderness in
The hand of whom you are walking.

Searching your purse to find a coin
To give to a disposed brother.

Preparing a special meal to share
With family, friends and others.

Love can be complicated when
Defusing a quarrel between brothers.

Love reminds us to be patient and kind
And keep step with our brothers.

Love is found in special things
Like greeting the morning sun.

Saluting the evening rain while
Tending your garden patch.

Love is the miracle which makes
Things happen and your garden grow.

Love honours your achievements
And sympathies with your trials.

Love is the serenity with which
You meet your challenges and trials.

Love projects your inner beauty
Of sparkle and grace and joy.

Love delights in your goodness
And the graciousness of all.

Love is that greeting and smile to
The elderly sitting outside the home.

Love is the pleasure in their smile
When they returned the greeting.

Love is present wherever you are,
Expanding the heart to embrace more.

Love is the attention and focus you give
To the good you do and what you say.

Love multiplies as you divide and
Share and grant each his due.

Love limits expectations of those
Incapable of delivering the more.

Love performs in subtle attention of
Feeding the hungry and the poor.

All around are opportunities to love
Not hidden in secret places.

Simple things giving pleasure is love.
Love is transferred one to the other.

Juxtaposed as we are on this planet,
Love can be here, there and anywhere.

As of today, see love in all things.

Ask and Receive

You must ask for what you want.
Not just sit around and pout,
As though waiting for some deliverance,
As though waiting for your salvation.

You must ask for what you want.
Do not fuss and fret and despair,
Worry and anxious about tomorrow.
Your needs are already known.

You must ask for what you want.
There is power in words.
So, give voice to your desires
With fervent pray and humility.

You must ask for what you want.
Believe yourself truly deserving.
Strongly visualize it is already yours
And graciously accept your gift.

You must ask for what you want.
   Just do what's asked of you.
Although not very special,
   Your help is on the way.

You must ask for what you want.
   And know your needs are already met.
There is one ever waiting to fulfil
   All wishes destined for you.

Just ask, believe and receive.

Grace

An undercurrent of power,
Seeping stealthily
Through time, aero, space and bower
And connecting calmly
In an undulating flow of oneness.

A sensing, as yet unperceived
By frightened souls, still deceived,
That all be borne of pain.
And nature in confusion reign
And so, fulfil her strangeness?

She brings to us grace of sharing,
Regardless of interest waring
And men with strengthened bond
Seeking changes, can be found
A source of abundant goodness.

Gifts of healing, she dispenses,
Opening hearts to break down defences,

Transforming obtuse dispassionate
Into gentle, kind and compassionate
To share in ever blissfulness.

For those who walk the path of faith,
Feeding off the enlightened saithe,
Success comes in peaceful measures,
With mellow touch and loving treasures,
A life encased by joyousness.

Creativity

Creativity has its source in divinity.
A universal pool of depth and infinity
Spreading widely and inexhaustibly.
Forever replenished. Never empty.

Divinity is ever ready to distribute
Generously as a means of retribute
To those courageous to contribute
To a stream preventing destitute.

Creativity is the gift of creation,
Designing and building its invention,
Organizing and moving into action
And fine arts in lively participation.

Gifts of creation profuse the pool.
The pool never obliterates new tools.
Never rejects nor discards old goods.
Makes anything possible out of wool.

Ideas are performed into unforgettable.
The new transformed into the possible.
The normal transferred to extraordinary.
Your desires fulfilled accommodatingly.

Creativity provides most of your needs.
Some freedom to be widely imaginative,
Freedom to conjure your where with all
And methods to procure and apply them all.

Generosity a guiding principle of creativity,
Provides abundantly for all activities.
The more you take, the more lavishly it gives.
So, deep in, take your fill and be creative.

Consciousness

Whatever is said and done
Will not detract you
From your ultimate fate.
Only you can change the tide of your life.

That troubling thought persists.
What is it saying to you?
Acknowledge it is there.
Pay attention, learn from it.
The new thought supersedes the old
The old thought is gone!

Stop beating up yourself.
Treat yourself with loving kindness
And accelerate the stream of perfectionism
Which you are continuously riding.

Do not abuse yourself.
Be gentle
And treat others as you
Would have them treat you.

We are in this world
To learn and grow.
And if you wish
You can learn from us
What we have learned from others.

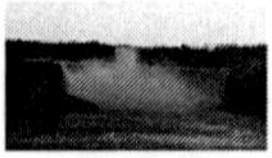

Genius is a dedicated performance
In response to God's gift of creation,
So endowed when the call is answered.
Just recognize and accept it.
Success is a gift that multiplies
When championed by brothers and sisters.
So endowed when approached.
Spread and speak of your brothers' genius.

Joy, Joy, Joy

How do I experience joy?
When do I express joyfulness?
Oh joy! Absolute divine joy!
My soul sings in blissful silence
Its tuneful rhythm of life.
My spirit dances to its
Vibrant pulsation of love.

A heart full of gratitude
Sings joyously of gladness.
And mindful appreciation
Dances gayly with goodness.
To live, to love, to sing,
To dance away the perils
of days long gone.

The present, this moment,
The now, lingers on and on,
Flows into the next moment
Of joy, of peace.
So, commence the songs
Of silence, of bliss,

So continues the dance
Of love and life.
So fills my being with joy.

The Holy Spirit

The Holy Spirit guides my ways
Purely to avoid me pain,
Mainly to protect my gains.

The Holy Spirit throws some light
To keep all daytime bright
And shine throughout the night.

The Holy Spirit harmonies my life
To balance its phases
And sing out its praises.

The Holy Spirit speaks its truth
To those willing to obey
Or prefer their own way.

The Holy Spirit gives me beauty
To project my inner glow
And let my goodness show.

The Holy Spirit pours abundance
For my gracious acceptance
And my constant deliverance.

The Holy Spirit provides security
To protect my sanctuary
And maintain healthy mentality.

The Holy Spirit is all-knowing
Inspires me in rightful thinking
And guides me from wrong doing.

The Holy Spirit is love in divinity
Present now and in eternity
To lead me to posterity.

Spiritual Awakening

Flowing so dark and deep,
The river of my mind to keep.
I must cross, I must swim.
It beckons and I weep
To climb up steps,
Narrow, tall and steep.
I swim, I have crossed, I climb.
My spirit flees, my soul's asleep.

Long winds that quiet road,
Where nature peeps, yet no man treads
Where shadows play and moths abound
And squirrels hop on dewy ground,
I took a step. Retract that step.
Dare I to join the game of life
Where spirits fly and souls don't die?

They marched in shackles, chained, but one
Who knew life's rhythms must go on.
The others faced an uncertain fate,
Deep longing etched their anguished face.
'Till freedom, peace and love awaking,

Broke loose their links, aware and seeking.
Their spirits flee, their souls asleep.

As I moved from dawn to dusk,
In a maze of darkened streams and streets,
In the distance, illumed by light
Nature’s toys on merry-go-rounds.
Must join the dance on the bright fair grounds.
Shed armour, shed shield, shed joyous tears.
My spirit flees, My soul’s asleep.

Spiritual Union

A kaleidoscope of pyrotechnics

Exploding at the centre of the soul,

Spreading blinking, twinkling, flickering lights

Throughout the entire being, the entire being,

Exciting every nerve, fibre and every tissue,

As each cell sparkles in glittering splendour.

A circadian glow of luminous spheres,

Smouldering in the heavens in rapturous ecstasy.

As the way is lit to guide the spirits on their

Soul searching journeys to revel in the delight

Of a sun, a moon, a ball of fire.

A radiance of bliss, a brilliance of joy!

A commingling of bright lights and

Loving spirits forming a spiritual union.

Purification

A deluge pounded the roof relentlessly,
Raining down steadily and furiously.
The skies parted; the heavens opened
Determined to shower its blessings
Even on those thought underserving.

I hurdled under warm cosy blankets,
Away from pealing thunderous clouds
And deafening racket of familiar noise
Of rain showers over streets and fields
Cleaning cutters, windows and doors.

Heavy turbulence just not at all inviting,
Pelting and pealing called to my being.
For a time thought I was underserving
And continued my hurdling and hiding
And listened to unrelenting downpouring.

Came out of hiding to watch the raining
Thinking it was heaven's blessings reigning.

As roads were cleansed by flowing water,
Time to go out get wet and shed my fear,
And request some cleansing and blessings.

Removed my clothes and ran outdoors.
Opening my arms and danced around
Allowing the showers to drench through
Revitalizing, reviving and regenerating
Like the green fields in their nourishing.

Danced some more, feeling wild and free
Like the roaring river disposing debris,
Sang out loudly and flushed my body
Washing loads of underserving stress.
Restoring, refreshing, purifying my spirit.

Playground of Dreams

Let us enter the playground of dreams,
Where anything is possible.
Fences have been removed.
All defences are down.
The space is open and inviting

Wide, wide open
And so, so inviting
It is open and inviting.
In the playground of dreams
We play and sing and dance.
In the playground of dreams
We love, we laugh, we cry.
The space is open and inviting

Wide, wide open
And so, so inviting.
It is open and inviting.
Boundaries are expanded
To infinite probabilities.
Horizons are extended
To limitless possibilities.

Much, much more open space
To do with what we will.

In this great space,
Everything is possible.
The space is wide and inviting.
I can plant my dreams
And watch them grow.
I remember the love and life
Of not too long ago
And give life to new loves
And love to new lives.
I create a new love.
I create a new life.

In that dream space,
I enjoy peace and truth.
Peace makes me myself
And makes me smile.
Truth leads me on.
I am me again,
renewed love, renewed life,
Peaceful and true
Playful, loving,
Focused, joyous.
I fill that open space.
I fill that dream space with me.

Life Purpose

Purpose is the time and space
Where deep gladness
Meets the world's great need.
The mind wants to know the time and space.

Deepest need and gladness come
From a place of love and loving.
We share all needs to be loved.
We join with all needs for loving.
Where the soul calls for this great love
The heart must follow.

The heart yearns to know,
The heart seems so hollow,
The soul cries out **move on!**
Just must go where it leads.
Never stop! Just follow.

The place is really undefined.
No signs to say stop and go.
The space is so unconfined,
Options to search and find.

There is no special time,
Only this moment here and **now.**
Open your eyes, expand your mind!
Listen to the sounds of your soul
Follow your heart, move forward in time.
There comes a time when all will settle.
Never look back, the dust will settle.
Desire will die, all is well.

Moving forward directs the purpose.
Ever flowing, it is never static.
It could be found everywhere,
Any place, any time, any dare,
In one move, in one action.

Learning and growing entice the motion,
Changing and increasing the station.
Be resolute in action for today,
Let completion be the goal.
Do not fret about tomorrow.
Tomorrow will take care of itself
Same resolve, same completion.

Life is a series of little motions
Coagulating into large notions.
No need to build big actions.
The little ones are just fine,
They are adequate for now.
The little ones will serve you well.

Tread lightly and confidently.
No need to be too careful,
No need to be too cautious,
Your needs will be revealed
As you move along your path.

Speak, sing, dance and be joyous!
Continue learning and plant your garden.
That is your soul purpose on earth.

The Teacher Learner

A perpetual learner

Always needs a teacher.

Still so much to learn

That everyone is a teacher.

The more we learn

The more there is to learn

So, enlist ourselves as teachers.

We are the teacher learners.

Knowledge buried in the past

Recalled only when needed.

For some, teaching years are dwindling

But learning must continue.

How can we learn with no teacher?

When the mind stops demanding,

Then learning days are ending.

And teaching time is done.

The teacher is indeed the learner.

Heart's Desire

I dillied and I dallied.
Said "yes!", said "no!"
Did this, that and the other,
Never what my heart truly desired.

I trembled in my shoes.
Whispered through my speech.
I walked with my head down.
Arms covering my breasts,
Holding secret my heart's desire.

It's time to reveal the secrets
Well-guarded for so long.
I did not trust myself,
Nor did I trust anyone else
To divulge my heart's desire.

How will my story be told,
If I am unable to unfold?
My heart desires to explore,
But my heart is a prisoner of my head.

If my heart is kept in chains,
No courage to unleash the reins,
Nor patience to unravel the brain,
Nor strength to uncover the drain.
Who will I be?
I will be nothing!
Like I started off to be. No thing!

Will I be content to be nothing,
Like before I emerged as a being?
When my head was just developing
And my heart was already forming?

My head says, "I'll never be content
To revert to nothing before birth."
My heart says, "Desires already
Existed long before the birth."

My head wants to be born again,
To experience a new beginning
And express its own beingness
Speaking of the heart's neediness.

My heart wants to take a fresh stance,
Seeking to reclaim its rightful dominance.
Head and heart are in sync for renewal.
Open up, accept and release their plural.

Desires correlate for a new beginning.
Heart leading head in its curriculums,
Head taking cues from heart inspires,
Doing what my heart now truly desires.

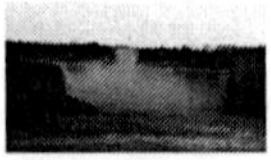

Public Life

A paradox of complexes

Wishing what is, should not be
And wanting the unavailability.
Like a noose is the credence,
That parenting is an accident
To be thoughtlessly regarded.
Parentage carelessly executed,
And may easily be discarded.
Being born to a specific heritage,
Gives rise to some vain prestige,
That asserts rights to advantages
Reserved for restricted parentage.
Whether parents are chosen or not,
You have exactly what you've got.
Love, guard, cherish and be happy.
What was given is no mistake.
It belongs to you now and forever.
Searching for other parents will never
Replace the gift of a loving mother
And the loss of an absent father.
You have no choice in the matter
Of sacred unity so closely familiar.

A pyramid of aspirations

As to where they fit in the
Hierarchy of class. Some
See themselves as belonging
To a superior class and will
Not welcome intruders.
Some aspire to a sect closed
To newcomers – les nouveaux
Riches. Some are eager to
Accelerate their entry to a
Higher class with much
Opposition. Few are content
To live simply, accepting
Their lot in life. While another
Few plod on slowly with
Seeming discontent and
Maladjustment. All are of
Honourable birth and worthy
Of their authentic beingness.

Misunderstanding of extroverts

Who love to hear their own noises,
As they loudly blare their voices.
Their emotions, thoughts and feelings
Are expressed in gregarious doings.
Their wish is to be noticed and

Admired for bombastic behaviours,
As they move on their carefree ways
And flaunt their thoughtless byways.

A longing by the introverts

Who remain too long behind
Bounds and scenes of obscurity.
Time to open up in observable
Sympathy. Commingle with
A community which will
Appreciate and listen to their
Inner cries for vivacious release,
Shed myths of shyness and timidity
And be allowed to express joyfully
What is conceived internally.

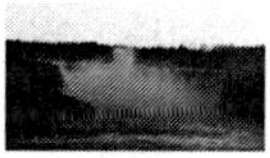

A subtle quarrel among religions

Establishing rites of due diligence,
Favouring one sect above the other.
Most religious persons walk these paths,
Faith in a heavenly eternal life,
Hope for a happy and successful now
And a long and prosperous tomorrow.

But first, we must learn to cultivate
Peace and learn to love and accept
Ourselves as we strive for a better life.
Then cultivate peace among others,
Who hope for the beautiful eternal life.
Let us be in sympathy with each other
As we speak to the Supreme God who
Answers when we each do our part.

Discordance between political factions

As they decide the good for their nation.
They honourably discharge their duties.
Admirably conspire to continue studies.
Commendably inspire mentoring subjects.
Hopefully and usefully crafting probabilities.
And instituting worthy workable policies.
Some may eliminate useless rhetoric
In favour of meaningful action. This
Could leverage their actions positively
And put them in advantageous positions
To later serve their communities.
While patiently waiting for the opportunity
To promote a progressive and just society.
And develop their own personal power.

An appreciation of culture

Long developed in nature
To grow, ease and mature.
Traditions handed down
From generation to generation,
Supporting the many expressions
Of food, clothing and shelter,
Of music, song and the dancer
Imbued in the soul forever.
To all peoples, race and creed
Create enjoyment out of need
To ease the strain, then proceed
With all daily living as decreed.
Where we go, culture may follow,
It may be graciously borrowed
And sometimes willingly loaned,
But cannot be gifted nor transferred.
Let us all join the celebrations
Giving happenings expression,
Sharing the essence of liberation.
Our culture is a very precious gift
To be expressed and celebrated.

Eternal Love

You have loved and lost.
Mourning at your own cost,
Memories buried in the past
Your love will always last.
Let the memories rest.
They will serve you best
As you remain in the present.
Your love is not lost.
It's alive eternally.
In its indestructibility
It exists in eternity.
Love is Eternal.

Happiness

Happiness, you elude me too long.
You keep lurking in the background,
Playing hide and hard to be found.
When found, I cling on for dear life.
But like a slippery seal, you glide,
Obstructing my grip with every slide,
Making it hard to retain my strides.

Finding you, caused some elation,
Thinking we had a good relation
As you lingered around for a while,
To maybe find real pleasure in time,
Not a tasty tease of what might be.
Desperate and frantic to keep alive,
What seemed like happy, had just died.

I am now beginning to understand
What happiness is and comes about.
The sometimes tease is unsustainable
And requires something maintainable.

Searching around grasping at straws
To find satisfactory adequate source,
And one who could be the true cause.

Happy seems related to cause and kin.
And only comes when they are invited in
To enjoin and enhance its infectiousness
And discard current states of seriousness.
For happy to sustain everlasting effect,
And maintain its crucial mode of infect,
Certain conditions must always be met.

Much happens to cause unhappiness.
These can be assessed by mindfulness,
To persuade thinking to one of gladness.
We may be daily grateful for aliveness,
And open the heart to give forgiveness.
Respond to trials with peacefulness,
Retaining a positive attitude of hopefulness.

Unwelcome unpleasantness is inevitable
Causing thoughts and feelings disagreeable.
But we are deserving of a joyful spirit,
And must quickly disclaim thoughts of dispirit.
Just acknowledge our rights to better life
By an understanding of how, what and why
To regain that infectious happiness drive.

Disagreeable situations cause malaise.
Moods of well-being can take a wide swing
By thoughts of discontent and inadequacy,

Feelings unloving, ungrateful and insufficiency.
And come back to centre by way of healing arts,
Such as singing, dancing, painting, drawing,
Writing, cooking, exercising and meditating.

Where persons are not involved as cause,
And goods not sourced as gain to retain,
But to extend the enhanced enjoyment team,
And alleviate impending unhappiness stream,
We employ simplicity, serenity and tenacity,
Together playing, praying, purling, partying,
With a steady daily dose of positive thinking.

Happiness is an inner state of contentment
As we approach life with commitment.
Receiving, giving, willing, undemanding,
Gracious, joyous, curious, spontaneous,
And conduct ourselves with thoughtfulness.
These are the main conditions demanded
With conscious effort to maintain the dream.

The dream is contained in various acts,
Changing tact to include your crafts,
Adopting a pet, delight in its grooming,
Joining a club, participate in its doings,
Volunteering in a community's accounting,
Learning something new and being curious.
Engaging hobbies may defuse the spurious.

Happiness, I am finding you, at last,
Moving through the inner journey pass
To contently dwell in my internal grasp
For healing, surrendering and loving.
When I sense you want to go into hiding
I pull out my happy thoughts for rhyming
Making sure your conditions are timing.

Searching for God

I seek You, Oh God, in solitude.
Alone, I know not where to turn,
But with much weeping and sighing
I speak of this emptiness.
This void that only You can fill.

I walk in shadows, scary and dark.
My life, I need must fill with light.
Who can help, themselves have lack.
You know of this emptiness.
This void that only You can fill.

Why chose me to come, Oh God!
What purpose must this life fulfil?
The pain stops only briefly
To ease into deeper and bigger pain.

I sometimes wonder, am I sane?
Why seek that which is unattainable
When around me, I see much strain
Mirrored in the unfathomable.

Why are humans so unkind?
Oh God, only You can tell.
Greed keeps getting bigger
Causing us to horde and hide,
Cheat and steal from each other.

Why can't we share with brothers?
Disowned like displaced creatures,
Black among white, red, yellow and brown,
We all belong! Oh! if we could only see
Indeed, we are all one.

Spontaneity

That was a curious movement,
Unexpected.
Reminiscent of another time.

A remarkable reaction of shock,
Convulsed
Shivers coursing through my spine.

Body tightening in anticipation.
Spontaneity
A goosebumps-raising infection.

Spontaneity knew no bounds.
Petrified
Didn't know why he came around.

Paused so close like the last time.
Nervous
Didn't know how to respond.

The drama needs an opening.
Watching
We are all watching and waiting.

All happening in record time.
Unpredictable!
Fast thinking and clever moves.

Responding to a pleasantry, he
Moved.
Like a panicked mouse, I scurried off.

Maybe he changed his mind.
He just wanted to be kind.
His act of goodwill,
Quelled my act of no will.

Me, Myself and I

A self-absorbed notion
You are thinking, believing
That anything I say or do
Is only about me for myself
And nothing to do with you.

With you alongside me,
We co-exist with them.
That's what matters more.
We are all in this together.
We need to support each other.

Aided by your assistance,
Guided by my willingness,
Aware of pain and darkness,
Together we can support them.
But first let us help ourselves.

The dictum of me, myself and I
Desires to create something
Valuable to offer you, but first

I must figure out who am I.
Who dwells within this dictum.

I am a casing for briefly
Housing myself and mine.
The casing can be fragile,
Easily blown away by vile
Storms of debris and guile.

Debris must be disposed,
Making way for the salvaged.
The salvaged must be restored,
Refurbished and renewed.
Ready for a new enhanced space.

Ferocity of storms cause terror.
Environments dark with horror,
Ambience dense and distressing.
Requiring resolve to clear the air,
Make clean and fresh and dear.

Some storms are unwittingly
Caused by you, me, anybody.
Storms leave damages and cost
Which could take a lifetime to
Repair or replace the loss.

Costs and loss may be mitigated
By awareness a storm is brewing.

Best to deal with by determining
Whether to deflect or accept.
Either way is your best interest.

Accepting a storm is to ride it
Expecting that it will soon pass.
Deflecting is to see it coming and
Move, allowing its spend to outlast.
Actions deliberate and intentional.

Deliberate action requires firm
Attention to the impending situation.
Accomplishment is imperative that
The whole being is entirely in sync
To respond to the circumstances.

I have weathered some storms.
Getting some bruises and rust.
I constantly nurse myself,
Clean up the residual mess,
Then prepare for the next test.

If the mess is unremoved,
Healing becomes tenuous,
Forgiveness often tedious.
Therefore, it is contingent on
Me to return to wholeness.

Storms forever brew around me.
Cleaning is an ongoing activity
Requiring constant proclivity.

To clear debris and futility,
I must employ my sensibility.

Awareness informs understanding.
Healing aids attention to clearing.
Cleansing the spirit brings forgiveness
Sensibility creates values transferable
Willingly offered to our co-existents.

Where we have done our own clearing,
Where we have done our own forgiving,
When we have done our own cleansing,
We can together work to fortify those
Caught in storms of their own dealing.

Mission of Faith

My life is a mission of faith.
The mission is long and tenuous.
My faith is subdued and dubious.

Lonely is that tortuous lane.
Strenuous is the tedious walk.
Treacherous the mountain top,
Thickets bushy and profuse
Line wide valleys and ridges.
Who will walk the thick and thin
Icicled gorge of cold streams?

Somewhere deep down,
The way leads on,
But I know not where.
My footsteps are slow
As I sometimes fear.
The way is spiral,
Round and round,
Higher and higher,
Yet as it gets rounder and higher
It moves down deeper and wider.

I sigh for the ordinary,
The easy, the touchable.
Destiny is so elusive.

My purpose so undefined,
But I have now learned
Where this mission leads.
Destination the only certainty.

As I sigh, I hear silent words,
'Your vision is clear and bright.
Your path is straight and right,
Do not stop your mission,
There is no turning back
Continue on your path.
I'll always be near!'

I disowned disbelief
As my journey continued.
My trust increased
As I saw the views promised.
A journey well-travelled,
Pulsing out with life.
A mission well enlivened,
Springing from all sides.
A heart well enlightened,
Shining out full bright,
Towards a mission of joy.

A joy within reach,
A mission sublime,
A faith not far behind,
Knowing that soon
I will arrive. I will arrive.
Now is the time of arrival.
Each step is arriving
Every path is the way.
And I am here.
My mission is done.
My faith fulfilled.

Talent

Talent is graced by creativity
And emerges from a curiosity
To know all about subjectivity.

Persisting with the activity
For testing your own alacrity
In the working of objectivity.

Applying your creative skills
To figure how it best works
And improving on what exists.

Tenacity to develop the subject
To the extent of all possibilities
Bringing it to full completeness.

What is subjected to excellence
And executed with persistence,
Is your chosen gift of talent.

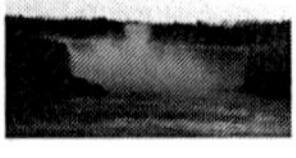

Prayer of Faith

I shall open my heart to the Lord
And beg His mercy and forgiveness,
And as His loving child
I shall be exalted.

I shall call out to the Lord
To release my grief and suffering,
And in His tender compassion
He will heal my pain.

I shall lift my hands to the Lord
For His richness in graces,
And like the great God that He is,
He shall pour out His spirit.

I shall open my mind to the Lord
To lead me in my ways,
And like the good shepherd that He is,
He will lead and guide me.

I shall walk with the Lord
And gladly embrace His goodness
And like the joyous deity that He is,
He will cherish my efforts.

I shall cry out to the Lord
And sing His praises
I shall listen to His teachings,
And bless His name forever.

I shall pray to the Lord
In humble meditation
And like the generous giver of all,
He will grant my needs.

Fantasy

Fantasy in all your beauty and zeal,
Would want me to believe you are real.
You create flights of fancy like floating
On cloud nine to build a pie in the sky.
Images wildly entertaining, but just
Beautiful flights of fanciful dreaming.

Fantasy in all your romantic ardour,
Stroll through the maze to dodge dour,
Dropping perfume on blooming flowers
Throughout the entire enchanted bower.
Then making daisy chains for your lover
Promising him undying love forever.

Fantasy in all your glamour and light,
Carouse jovially like Gadsby's delight
And own a yacht in the South of France.
Amidst a kaleidoscope of a gay prance,
Sparkling, shining, twinkling and bright,
Wishing to have wings and fly all night.

Some fantasies are only wild imaginings
And are not grounded in reality.
Some are daydreaming thoughts of fancy
That must at one time accept the reality
That what is fancied may be an impossibility.
Or given a purpose to become a true reality.

Since my thoughts create my life reality,
I am reluctant to conjure new fantasies,
For fear they will become my reality.
Because some thoughts can be fanatical.
So, I have to be careful what I fantasize,
Keeping them to the good to materialize.

Some fantasies are seen for what they are,
Just mere daydreaming uncharacterized
And can quickly evolve into merchandise.
Some are repetitive and become obsessive.
The pleasure of it remains constantly active,
Still clinging relentlessly on being addictive.

Some regret to have taken it seriously.
Such a fable can send you up deliriously
And bring you down low dispassionately.
Such fantasies become persistent desires
That have the knack for being consistent
Until unfulfillment leads to resentment.

Long outstanding fanatical desires
Rest forever on mental screen spires.
Languishing in expectation to materialize.

These can be prompted with realistic attitudes
And treated with positive mental capabilities
To hopefully emerge as possibilities.

Some fantasies can change to realities,
When dynamically programmed for activities.
Fancy visions of extraordinary stained glass
Were replicated on church window blasts.
Images of holy sacred scenes were interpreted
On the ceilings of the Cistern Chapel dais.

Dream design revelations are enacted
In fashions and homes and gardens and halls.
Transformational ideas are made into inventions
Of tools, technologies, trinkets and toys.
Intuitions transport the growing modern trends
And move them into popular directions.

Imagination guides the creation of music,
And choreographs movement and dance.
Fantasies are an important part of living,
When they move us to create profusely,
Perform that which are extraordinary, and
Innovate the strange and unimaginable.

Some pursue their fantasies relentlessly.
And live them out with grandiosity.
Procurement of a vacation home in Biarritz,
Yachting year-round and entertaining friends.
Some acquire a chateau in North Italy
Amidst large vineyards for exquisite wines.

She fancied residing in an ancient castle.
And ended up in Eze, off Monaco strip,
Selling high-end goods in the castle caves.
A country cottage was her ultimate desire
Where she could totally relax close to her dyer.
She now produces colourful clothing for hire.

Today, he is a world-renowned surgeon,
Who had made paper runs to meet his legion.
A boy's life long fantasy becoming a reality.
With spontaneity, playfulness and dedication,
A mind focused on achieving its aspirations,
A fantasy can indeed become an actuality.

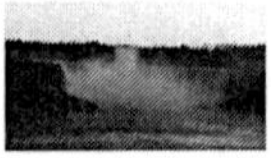

T'ai Chi

They tell me
T'ai Chi is
Poetry in motion.
Movements emanating
From the spine,
A sit, open up
A stand, then down.
Like the ebb and flow
Of waves,
Merging yin and yang;
Fusing the
Anima and animus;
Spirit and Soul.
All converging
In oneness.

When motion is
Superimposed by words,
Rhythm and melody,
This becomes
Poetry of love.
Pen and mind

Inspired by the Chi.
The Christ energy
Completely takes over
Putting together words,
Music and song.

When you see a dance,
Know it's T'ai Chi,
The way of energy,
Poetry in motion,
Dipping, tipping, sitting,
swinging,
Twisting, twirling, turning
Waving, holding, grasping,
Delighting, enchanting
Inspiring and merging with
The Christ energy,
Poetry of love,
Words, rhythm and song
culminating in the dance
of life.

Homecoming

(Wholeness)

I looked at my face in the mirror.
Scrutinized every crease and mole.
Examined their reasons for being.
Wondered whether they tell a tale,
Signs of my life journey detailed.

Not showing many creases and lines.
Maybe because of my family binds.
Everything not recorded externally,
But be sure that what is not external
May be internal, emotional or mental.

Can't refute what brought me here.
Have suspended my trials and fear.
And championed successes and gains.
I scoured my memory for lingering pain,
Which did not come readily to reign.

I think I am on my way to recovery.
Maybe moving towards home discovery.
I no longer import nor do I succumb to

Other people's insecurities and pain,
When infused left me very little to gain.

I peered in the mirror for a closer look.
Searching eyes for a glimpse of my soul.
I wanted to know my level of growth.
Had I progressed and achieved my goal
Of healing, forgiving and being whole?

They say the eyes are windows of the soul.
The soul revealed what was overlooked,
Some additional stories for another book.
An already overcrowded disposition
With issues needing new directions.

Brokenness not completely mended,
So many issues needing forgiveness.
There is still so much work to be done.
It seems that my work has just begun.
Needing courage for the coming run.

Takes tenacity to deal with brokenness,
Accept healing as a continuous process.
Dealing with situations crossing our paths,
Requires goodwill so they will not last
And bring us home with little malaise.

Be mindful of what should be exercised.
Acceptance and compassion towards
Neighbours so kind and accommodating,

Treated with disdain and condescension
for their simplicity and meekness.

They went out of their way to be gracious.
Their preferential attitude was treated
Carelessly and received nonchalantly.
It needed flexibility and consideration.
All are deserving of loving kindness.

Where the treatment was discourteous,
And lacking in human considerations,
That was their painful call for love
And should be responded with forgiveness.
Forgiveness for them and for oneself.

These are the needs for wholeness.
Working towards wholeness is lifelong.
When you no longer see brokenness in
Your brother, nor brokenness in yourself,
You will finally be approaching wholeness.

Wholeness is impossible to achieve, for
It exists in its entirety only in selflessness.
Complete healing is ultimate wholeness.
As we continue our work of perfection,
We are nearing the glorious homecoming.

Relationships

Life

Life what a cruel game you play,
Giving with one hand and
Pulling it back with the other.
As though if we want the whole,
We must work smarter to recover.
As though to recover the whole,
We would have to work stronger.

Life what a tricky stance you take.
You promised me happiness as I make
Cuddly moves in my mother's sake.
Getting the feeling that sometimes
All was not too well on the outside
And would have to pretend to hide,
Growing cosy and happy on the inside.

Life what a devious plot you weave.
You returned as unwanted my gifts
Of food, of clothes, goods and things.
You refuted my knowledge and skills,

As not currently requested nor needed.
You revoked my tender broken heart
Replacing it with compassionate acts.

Life what a merciless deal you make.
You seem displeased whenever I shake,
As I dwell in the seeming happy past
And bring with it the unfortunate last.
How you weld that cruel brutal stick
To keep me right on track and unstuck
Motivating me to aspiring streaks.

Life what heartless tasks you command.
Dissatisfied with all I do and demand,
Repeat drudgery of cooking and cleaning,
As though not enough, eating and drinking.
You compel my sloth to exercise and play
Pushing introvert talk and smile to sway
Propelling me out of my comforting way.

Life what forgiving tributes you grant.
What will you have me do that you want?
Unless to say that I have done it all and
Your wish for me is, now just learn to be,
Surrender and allow you to guide me
To ride the tides of what's left of me.
You always wanted the very best for me.

Life, I have at last got your measure.
Living always to deliver your treasures.
You have sustained me thus far, But
It is up to me to listen to your voice.
Moving in time to the inner drums
Beating out peace, love, surrender
Changing tact to carry me yonder.

Inclusivity

Do not remain aloof
 And stand apart.
Be visible and be seen.

Join in the conversation
 And say your part.
Be present and listen.

They are talking about you,
 This, that and the other.
Listen with your heart.

Grasp the unknowing.
 Savour the moment
As it comes to pass.

This time of wisdom
 Coming so rarely
Will not trespass.

Let your spirit show
  With fire and passion
Express yourself to grow.

Be there in person
  Supportive and kind.
Allowing yourself to shine.

So bright as to dazzle
  Lighting the way to
Keep a step with your brother.

Be totally inclusive
  Not lose sight of each other
We're all in this together.

Emotional Intelligence

In the workplace was a scene,
Like I had never before seen.
Ranting and raving all about.
Yelling and running all around.
As though only chaos reigned.
They all seemed to have lost control.

The ranting was a misunderstanding
That directions were not clearly given,
And was causing much confusion.
They raved that happened too often
And cannot be allowed to continue.
These issues really needed correction.

The yelling was who was right or wrong
And could be stopped by intervention.
The running in all directions was like
Putting out fires to lessen combustion.
Who was the one inciting the chaos?
Why was there such a loss of control?

There were questions to be answered.
There were subjects to be covered.
There was organization to execute.
There was management to educate.
All demanding emotional intelligence
And getting everyone back in line.

A calm followed a general meeting.
Communication skills were examined
To lessen the incidence of disputes,
And ensure directions efficiently given,
The method of employees' reporting
To make for more harmonious relating.

They reviewed the organization structure,
Equitable placement of persons to ensure.
Off-site learning for staff was promised.
Individual personal coaching committed
To determine and strengthen soft skills
And balance emotional intelligence.

Personal coaching was very beneficial,
Increasing self-awareness and motivation.
Affirming what is already there and
Brainstorming to commit some more,
Self-confidence to perform the test
And belief in producing the very best.

With the merging of emotion and intellect,
Assurance of intelligent balance creates
An affable atmosphere in the workplace,
And a congenial productive staff relationship.
Performances are proficient and competent.
And the organization experiences high returns.

With astute leadership assessing competencies,
Eliciting equitable benefits and rewards and
Encouraging further education and skills,
Willing employees can accomplish their goals.
Performing at their optimum, adhering to
Policies and culture, all converge as winners
By an infusion of emotional intelligence.

Liking

Do not be complacent
About your likes.
Enquire within.
See what you like
And strengthen the findings in yourself.

Do not be offended
About their dislikes.
Examine your deeds.
See what you have done
And quell the findings within yourself.

Disavow yourself of this notion,
Liking this and disliking that.
Tread lightly with an open mind.
Liking enhances intimacy.
Disliking heightens sensibility.

Do not be so deceived,
Lest the truth be known
Buttons pressed unconsciously,
When you discover dislikes
Are simply resentments.

Your wish to like
When enquired within will become
Admiration and inspiration,
A companionship of new liking.
Dislikes are truly your likes.

Tes Kawants

{Wayward Boys}

Enrolled in public primary schools,
In Islands' town and country rooms,
Tes kawants attended schools on a whim,
Between many adventurous themes.
Priority for that day, their freedom.

Non-school attendance was not always
A desire to run wayward elsewhere.
They needed to spend time somewhere
Searching for sustenance to supplement
Meagre portions doled the night before.

The meal came straight from the field.
There they exercised forbidden choices,
Using sling shots as weapons of choice.
Shot birds, downed mangoes with stones
And on the way raided fruits for lunch.

Tes kawants were very resourceful.
Took their meals wherever they could,
Sneaking through windows to claim a tasket,

Pinching bread off a neighbour's basket
To appease their growing hunger pangs.

School attendance required full attire
Not feet shod and threads fit to retire.
So, they stayed away roaming thread bare
Until they acquired hand-me-down wears.
To at least look decent like other boys.

Bayfront, riverbanks, roadsides and parks
Were their hangouts in daylight and dark.
Their main occupation teasing passers-by
While calling out to colleagues in crime
Daringly urging them to perform malign.

What utter freedom tes kawants enjoyed.
They stripped off rags at weekly sea docks,
Opening their arms and riding the waves.
They preferred Sundays for river head dives.
Yelling, pushing and teasing anyone nearby.

The wayward boys were very inventive.
Using corn beef cans and glory cedar sticks,
As they challenged their skills in cart building.
Competing dexterously avoiding some nicks.
Imitating racing cars' movements and tricks.

Their favourite sport was driving a seck,
A bare bicycle wheel guided by a stick.
The beauty of movement was multitasking,
Holding up dropping pants like one asking,
While rolling the seck wheel for the basking.

Tes kawants' minds could not fathom
Normal lessons in a regular classroom.
Their main education was street smarts
Learned in common market place darts
Listening to gossip, news and prates.

They expressed themselves nonchalantly.
Freedom in speech, manner and deed,
Opinions uninvited, unafraid, open and wild.
They flaunted a sacaboy swagger in stride
And a teasing demeanour as their pride.

A general nuisance was their major vice.
Bombastically clever dodging police.
They deflected cuffs like in boxing camps
Declaring themselves true MVP champs.
To the amusement of curious passers-by.

Some seemed to have abandoned school.
With minds focused on some sort of work,
They took small jobs wherever they could.
Their main goal to get a bebop haircut,
Coco-piece pants and polyester collars up.

Some talk animatedly of future plans.
So, sometimes pop in a classroom to
Grasp the minimum learning stance.
Some roam about taking life askance.
A jockey blusters their main advance.

Freedom and openness favoured them,
With confidence to be themselves.
Some recognized their inadequacy
And resumed learning at evening dates
In anticipation of good pay rates.

Some with additional class learning
And street-smart knowledge craving
Held argumentative positions everywhere
Participating in all debates anywhere.
Taking the lead in developing anything.

Today, tes kawants are unrecognizable.
They have grown to be quite responsible.
Acknowledging that their early start,
Required extra effort in their current state
To be caring humans that they are today.

Tes kawants seriously executed leadership,
Extolling the discipline of education,
And values of honesty, integrity and attention.
They lived up to certain expectations
Of being role models for the nation.

Some continued waywardness in adulthood.
Plying cart service as means of livelihood.
Entertaining with carefree good humour,
An endearment to all who stopped and stared.
Tes kawants are such interesting personalities.

Imperfection

Everything comes from nothing.
A thought, an idea, a vision
Influenced by all around,
Enacted becomes a creation.
Creation gives life and
Meaning in all its complexities,
Inspires art.

Complexities by their very nature
Are imperfect.
How can we be assured the
Adaptations would be perfect?

Humans are born from
A thought, a desire, an action,
An act of creation, an individual.
Each holding its own
To retain its authenticity as it
Creates art.

People study art and nature
To capture their very essence.
A tweak here, a brush there,
Words of wisdom to
Understand art.

Art mirrors man.
Man is complex and not perfect.
Man influences art.
Therefore, art is not perfect.
Art records humanity.
There will be errors in the copying.
All a mesh mash, imperfect all.
Nothing is perfect!
No one is perfect!
Perfect exists only in the imperfect.

The Elites

You called out to him, *"You Boujwa!"*
What makes you refer to him that way?
Understand! you called that man *Accourase*
Because he welded a cutlass to cut grass.
Paypay Tongue with his enormous stutter
Started a sentence with a paypay utter.

But why do you call him *boujwa?*
How has he earned or disowned that name?
Does he answer to that title or not
Or connect with the little history put forth?
Don't psych up yourself to argue with me.
History writes itself for you and for me.

Before the fifteen-century phenomenon,
The world knew mainly farming for all.
Thus, survival of the fittest proved only
Those willing, able and strongest survived.
Fighting desperation and conquering lands
With loyal subjects, they divided the spoils.

The bold and masterful invented rules
To keep them all controlled and in check.
Flaring tempers which could not abide,
The rebellious, callous and full of pride
Were all banished from a growing class
To live elsewhere, populate and colonize.

You can now see with whom we share
Our deep-rooted origins of early peasantry,
A common ground of fertile soil
With popes, kings, queens and gentry,
Who made up rules and rued the day,
Banishing rebels to make their own way.

A banished class of European exiles
Got involved in the purchase of Africans.
Hailed from Africa's rich heritage, they
Came to the Islands *Negre et Negresse*
To couple with landed European whites
For a class of *mullato et mullatresse.*

What a melding of tones and sights,
Blending of white race with the black.
Infighting about who is lighter or dark.
The dark less privileged than the light.
The light must behave in such a way
Another mode of behaviour for the black.

Thus evolved the Island Creole net
With the already-established Kalinago set.
The culture was collectively enjoyed
As long as each person knew his place,
Did not intrude in each other's space.
And made no effort to further mix the race.

Five centuries later, a European sect,
Gained a place in history as a social class,
Started by Monsieur Bourgeois of France,
Bourgeois was raised in peasantry and trade,
Occupations rebuffed by the aristocrats,
But he was determined to face their autocrats.

Bourgeois with his like-minded colleagues
Excelled in industry, commerce and trade.
Great ambition and tenacious industrialism,
Monsieur Bourgeois backed by his enormous
Wealth, acquisitions and influence went on
A rampage buying everything they could.

They flaunted their new money to buy all,
And the indebtedness of failing aristocrats.
While moving up in the world as their own
With Bourgeois as lead to claim a class.
Tagging along only those of great wealth
Who could influence like *Les Bourgeois*.

Trying to buy the acceptance they wanted,
They changed their course, snobbing the past,
While fervently yearning ranks of aristocrats.

A privilege denied for their class imitation.
So, they took matters in their pecuniary hands,
And invented a new class *Les Bourgeois.*

Islanders are becoming more educated
With glowing careers branching in places.
Professions proudly extolled by families
Of farmers, traders, maids and labourers,
A generation or more of early peasantry.
No bourgeois existed here then and now.

You have gained insight of *Les Bourgeois.*
That eighteenth-century snobbish class
Of unsuccessful aspiring aristocrats
Could never infiltrate their values,
In an Island already so rich in culture
And confident in its social structure.

Why do you call him *"You Boujwa"*?
Because he seized opportunities?
You are endowed with similar capabilities.
Just look, learn and apply your abilities.
Islanders are already in a special class
Inventive, witty and smart as a rasp.

Why respond to the call *"Boujwa"*?
Do you wish it were a compliment?
Do you hope it can foster superiority
Or replenish the diluted nationality
By importing that ancient middle-class
To superimpose Island-grown personality?

Shed that coat which guards your thinking
And keeps you stuck in past reasoning.
You live in interesting progressive times
With much opportunity to rise and shine.
Polish up your present brilliant mind
That speaks so eloquently of other times.

Your individuality speaks to your authenticity.
You have earned your titles and your deeds.
Where you think you have further need,
Join colleagues in varying degrees.
Drop the complexes of multiple scales
And be promoted to the ranks of the *Elites*.

Siblings

Siblings have each other's
Best interests at heart.
Hearts that give generously
And take evasively.
They give strong opinions
And righteous indignation
If their interests are
Not in congruence.
And take off in a huff of
Embittered entitlement
When their interests
Are not met.

They make condemnations.
Defining actions as right
Or wrong as thou they
Were elected judge or jury
Over each other's actions.

Siblings claim they are
Always there for you.
But you had better

Be not too far when
Needed. Otherwise,
You'll forever be
Reminded and never
Hear the end of it.

Some siblings have missed
Their true calling in life.
Should have been
Preachers and teachers
Not sisters and brothers.
They overlook what's
Wrong for themselves
But always know
What's right for you.

What's right for you,
Is sometimes a wish
For you to live your
Best life based on their
Precepts of what that
Best life could mean.
Best lives take on
Different meanings
And need different
Directions. Siblings must
Decide which path
Best suits their direction
And follow that path.
Siblings must conclude
That each has to

Make his own way
To live that best life.
Therefore, we have to learn
To accept the other's
Decision and let go.

We have been given
Our own lot in life.
A life taking one direction,
While another's veer in
Another direction.
Each journey is special
And unique and should
Be respected as such.
Therefore, when
Your sibling goes his
Own way, he needs to
Take his path to fulfil
His purpose. Give him
Your blessings and
Love and accept him
Just as he is.

Siblings hold each other
To dubious standards.
Standards that say, "Do
As I say, but not as I do!"
This is not a deliberate
Ploy to deceive.
It is just abject
Unawareness of their

Way of being.
They have to apply
Mindfulness to practise
What they preach.
And watch more closely
Their sayings and doings.

A sibling unleashes
A firestorm of a tantrum,
Signalling to the other
That a behaviour left
Much to be desired.
Justifiable, that tantrum
Could mean fear for his
Sibling which ultimately
Could be fear for how the
Behaviour would impact
Him and others.
Tantrums may be childish
Behaviours to get attention,
Or express fears or caring.
Siblings may now realize
That a reasonable discussion
May be more persuasive
To clear the air.

Siblings truly have each
Other's interest at heart.
A warm heart that wants
To secure their happiness
And prevent them hardships.

Indeed, we are our brother's
Keepers and so, responsible
For each other. Like
The Buddhists, taking
Responsibility is being
Able to respond to
Each other's needs
And capabilities, not
Exert control over
Their thoughts and
Deeds, but empathize
With their feelings and beings.

Siblings' best interests
Diverge in all directions.
Trajectories guided
By their experiences
and different influences.
When we eventually
Bring all our experiences
And influences to bear,
We may enhance our
Learning and growing
And so, assist each
Other in meaningful ways.

When imparting
Information as yet
Generally unknown,
We have to be careful
To do so in helpful

Tones. We cannot know
Everything and it is
All right to share information.
But this should be done
With kindness and
Without condescension.

Criticisms diminish
Self-esteem. Some siblings
Believe that what they
Know is the ultimate
Truth and there's the
Only source of knowing.
All opinions are worth hearing.
Maybe by listening a little
Closely, something may be
Learned by the new information.

Supporting each other
Is very necessary.
Loyalty will help
Build confidence,
Further endeavours
And good intentions.
Sympathy will create
An understanding
Of what we can
Be to each other
And uplift each other
In trying times.

Siblings come out in
Full force and
Take up arms in support
Of each other when
Their general well-
Beings are threatened
By outside entities.
Don't play around
With them! they will
Not allow you to attack
A sibling without
Putting up a fight
To protect the other.
When all is said
and done, there is
No denying their loving
Bonds and underlying
Deep affection.
Siblings truly love each other.

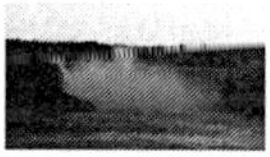

Aging

We did not know the joy of youth
Would not last forever.
We did not know that happiness
Would not repeat ever.
Every event is marked in time.
Never to come back again.
What's done is already done,
What's said has been said.
No going back. No taking back.

Do not think us ancient and raging
Because we sometimes talk of aging.
We were born, survive, then later die,
And other events in between.
The counting of age starts at birth
As we emerge from mothers' girth.
One minute, one month then a year,
Celebrating loves and lives throughout
As time piles up year after year.

They simply crept up without knowing.
Were we unmindful and not looking?
One day we were three just starting school,
Now we forget where we are going.
Such high numbers from where did they come?
Though we have been watching closely
They simply crept by leaps and bounds,
Not just adding year after year
But by multiples of decades all along.

Should not have accumulated so fast,
We scarcely turned our backs.
Suddenly, we are that unmentionable number,
Which have been avoided for decades
By clinging to the childish notions
That we will be young forever.
At this age today, our grandmothers
Were already old ladies. Are we old ladies
That we are now loathe to admit?

I met an old friend in the shopping plaza
Whom I had not seen in many decades.
We stared at each other to recall the other.
No recognition, then it suddenly clicked.
We had been best friends in elementary school.
"I am sixty-nine," she proudly said, defying
Her age. "Buying dye to colour my hair."
While she teased her sparse thinning hair
Which had seen several shades of grey.

One of my friends frequently asks,
"Do I need a colour. I don't like greys."
She has this obsession of not showing
Grey hairs and wants always to colour
Every one that shows its curious dour.
Her first question to acquaintances is,
"How old would you say I am?"
To get an answer she is ten years younger
To be assured of her sustaining looks.

They tell my friend she looks sixty-three
When, in fact she is almost eighty-three.
Persons treat their hair strangely.
Always fussing with and colouring them.
Today red, tomorrow blonde, brown next day,
"Does this look good. Can you see the greys?"
Covering the greys will not reveal the age.
The real age will be known in coming time
With the revelations for celebration of life.

I squirm when called mam or madam.
Feel I should defy these spouting youths
Prancing around in five-inch-high heels.
And non-existent cleavage from tank tops.
I look like my mother slow in aging.
She was proud that she looked like my sibling.
Remaining there, trying to smooth the wrinkles.
Grimacing in mirrors to see how they delay,
Responding to potions, lotions and creams.

Packing up the years, is an interesting time.
Didn't expect that in such a short while.
Feel blessed as I walk down the aisle,
Voice raised in song praising the Lord.
Feel respected and free when I take advantage
Of all discounts and choice places in lines.
Shamelessly hocking best seats at all times.
And continuing to stand while everyone sits.
That is a true sign of coming of age.

Values well ingrained and undisputed.
I love the me I am becoming.
Motives inscrutable in my poker face,
Don't know what I'll project next.
Only suspect it could be the best.
Feigning confidence in my staggering gait,
Hoping not to fall flat on my face.
Let's all continue to give ourselves approval,
Enjoy our last lap together as we come of age.

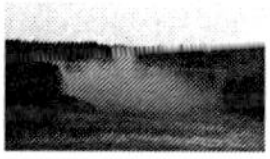

Romance

They snuggled together in the back seat
Savouring their love for each other.
The car gave them the closeness they craved,
With no breathing space between the other.
They took pleasure in their nearness and
Spent many happy hours together.

They walked hand in hand
Always looking for a spot
To cuddle and to stop.
Today, they chose a hotel
To spend the night
And wake in the morning
To break their fast.

They lingered in the subway.
Reluctant to say goodbye.
Hesitant to go their separate ways.
They wanted to sit there forever.
She clung to him, kissing anywhere
He held onto her, touching everywhere.
Will they ever break away and go home?

Her eyes searched the crowd.
She waited with baited breath
To catch a glimpse of him.
He moved through his peers,
Purposefully and expectantly.
When their eyes met saying, "I love you."
The message was unmistakable.

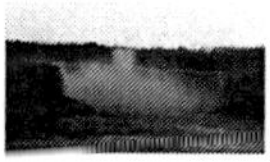

Music played. Friends swayed.
Heartbeats thrumming. His
Approach strutting dignity and grace
Such a handsome man.
Her one-time dear love.

Confidence in strides.
Elegance in manners.
Magnificent and upright
A smile on his face.
What an absolute joy to await
The love of her life.

The romantic soul yearns for lovers
And enwrap them in its warm embrace.
But lovers can scarcely be found.
They hide among materials,
Chasing after the more.
Preoccupied with the wanting and having.
Forgotten about the giving and being,
Misunderstanding the art of living.
The soul again wants that loving feeling!
The tenderness, the touch, the longing,
The look which says, “I love you.”
The love that sets the soul free to rejuvenate,
The spirit enthralled to express grandly,
The love to flow through all said and done.

Life Lessons

Ego and arrogance, hand in hand
You run amok,
Roaming wild and unchecked,
Treading on toes and crushing legs.
You are not so privileged!
It is time to change trajectory.
Apply the brakes, stay in line
And keep off the tracks of brutality.

When you walk in a place,
Prepared to criticize and
Make negative connotations,
You will miss the beauty of
God's creations expressed by
His willing subjects.
You were not elected judge
Over God's creations.

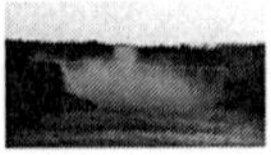

Speak good of others.
They have enough of the world's
Bad with which to contend.
They do not need more
Added to their portend.

Think that you have grown a lot,
In fact, you have grown just a tad.
It's a lifelong process
Which needs no regress.

When you offend unwittingly,
Give an apology willingly.
When you are due an apology,
Accept it graciously.

Be vigilant in what you say to a brother.
His life journey may be different from yours.
What he will meet on his path is unknown.

Tell him of your experiences
And allow him to make his own decisions.

Each day, give gratitude for all gifts
And blessings and trials received.
Gratitude for blessings livens your
Spirit in anticipation of a happy day.
Blessings for trials strengthen you
To meet whatever comes your way.
Gratitude for gifts opens your heart
And prepares you for receiving more.

You do not need everything.
Everything is not meant for you.
Do not covet your brother's property.
You do not know how he obtained it
And what he must do to retain it.

Let us each live the life that was given to us
And allow others to live theirs.

Our beauty, intelligence and grace
Shatter glass ceilings into millions of
Fragments spreading all over the universe.
See ourselves as sparkling stars
Of the glorious community of humans.

Do not leave without me,
Though you dwell in the shadows.
There must be light for your shadows
And your leaving obliterates the light.
If there is no light, there is no shadow
There can be no you without
The shadow and the light.

Life is a beautiful thing!
We have only one chance at it.
As of today, see it in all its glory
Ready to envelope us in its warm story.

Leave the broken past behind,
Engage in current time benign
And live each day in joy of the Divine.

An opinion is merely an expressed belief,
That sometimes draws its reasoning from truth.
The opinion may be accepted by an act of faith.
Or sometimes rejected in the absence of knowledge.
Truth dwells only in reality.
And fully experienced through the innate senses.
Therefore, there is no argument with truth.
And it should never be rejected.

The knack of keeping up with others,
Is to wear your own shoes.
The truth of holding up,
Is standing in your own shoes.
The beauty of your walk,
Is stepping out in your own shoes.

Humorous Moments

I sit around to recall humorous moments.
That in itself is already a hilarious event.
My mind goes blank, no jokes to conceive.
If I think harder maybe something will give.
My strong thoughts delay producing a line
If persistent, I know something will rhyme
And you'll find a joke to mark my time.

How long must I wait for that punchline
So easily delivered by most one lines?
My comedic claims are somewhat remiss
So, don't expect me to make you hiss.
A surprise burst of laughter follows when
I inventively dare say something unusual.
Was this really a joke to make you crawl?

Let me search my thoughtful of truths
To check for jokes or rumours untrue.
What is there might give you a thrill
And conjure images worth the telling.

I might talk of the visiting white dove,
Or defusing a quarrel between two loves
Or inebriated men staggering in droves.

I was telling my boyfriend about my dream
In which a handsome man with long legs
And dreamy eyes sat next to me on my bed.
I told the man, "I love your beautiful eyes."
In reply, he spontaneously kissed me.
Never had a kiss like this before and since.
The dream ended with the delivery of the kiss.

My boyfriend does not like to know I enjoy
Someone else's kisses better than I do his
And wanted to talk some more about this.
Thought a little teasing would put him straight
But he refuted that and refused taking the bait.
"I am only teasing you, love," I said
"That guy in the dream was no other than you!"

"Do not get jealous and upset about this.
It was you in my dream who delivered that kiss.
The deepest and sweetest I have ever had,
A gut-wrenching kiss that turned my head.
Would be nice though if you could replicate
In real-time what you do so well in my dreams.
What a glorious time we'd have together."

Want to hear other stories? some another time
When we might add opera singing in Rome
Or create other jokes as they come to mind.
Blank paper and pen are a very good start
To write down thoughts and wise sayings
And humorous moments as they come to pass.
Looking forward to entertainment that lasts.

Miramur – The Forest Nymph

(Mary's Carnival Queen)

Miramur, the forest nymph,
A flowering bred of exotic plant,
Grafted with hibiscus, orchids and rose,
She feeds off drips of rivulets and streams.
Nurtured by vibrant mountain breeze,
And warming kisses of the tropical sun.

In her plight for vision and growth,
Miramur springs slender and tall.
And effortlessly winds her way
Through multiple foliage of dates.
Prominently stands out, thinking
Herself, sole Goddess for all mates.

And as she flourishes, she drapes
Flowing circular train of forest green
Flounces and folds. And like magic,
Cleverly transforms greens into colours
Of her choosing, a gift from nature,
True colours of embroidered satin rose.

Miramur blossoms, as she sheds
Delicate sequinned leaves strewn abed.
She leaves in her wake, beautiful traces
Of finest, tiniest particles of rose dust.
As from herself emerges myriads of
Gayly dancing petals and twirls.

Puffed petals of pearls
Puffed petals of beads
Twirls of gold, green, pink and seeds,
Dripping from her off-shoulder deeds.
A dropping waist and pencil thin skirt,
Framed by iridescent sweetheart kerbs.

The happy nymph dances and sways
On graceful legs, with elegant gait,
She engages with her smiles and grace.
Charming many in her delightful space.
She springs alive in her fabulous looms
The smoothest, velvety satin blooms.

Radiantly exhibiting her talents on stage,
She dazzlingly outshines the other stars.
Personifying the magic of forest nymphs,
She captures the favourite of onlookers,
Availing herself of some present awards,
The winner, Miramur, Forest Nymph.

Glossary

Bebop	Hairstyle of the 60s
Boujwa	French patois for Bourgeois
Bourgeois	French social class
Coco-piece	Inexpensive fabric material
Elites	Leaders, best chosen/elected
Mullato	French for colored race – male
Mullatresse	French for colored race – female
MVP	Most Valuable Player
Negre	French patois for negro – male
Negresse	French patois for negro – female
Sacaboy	Nonchalant attitude
Tes Kawants	Little vagabonds